This is the house where
Julia lives.

Julia can see green fields
from the back of the house.

Julia drew this picture of her house.
She drew the rooms inside the house.

Roof

Bathroom

Kitchen and
Dining room

Front door

My home in a village

Julia lives in a small village
called Shudy Camps.
It is near Cambridge in England.
There are fields all around the village.

SHUDY CAMPS

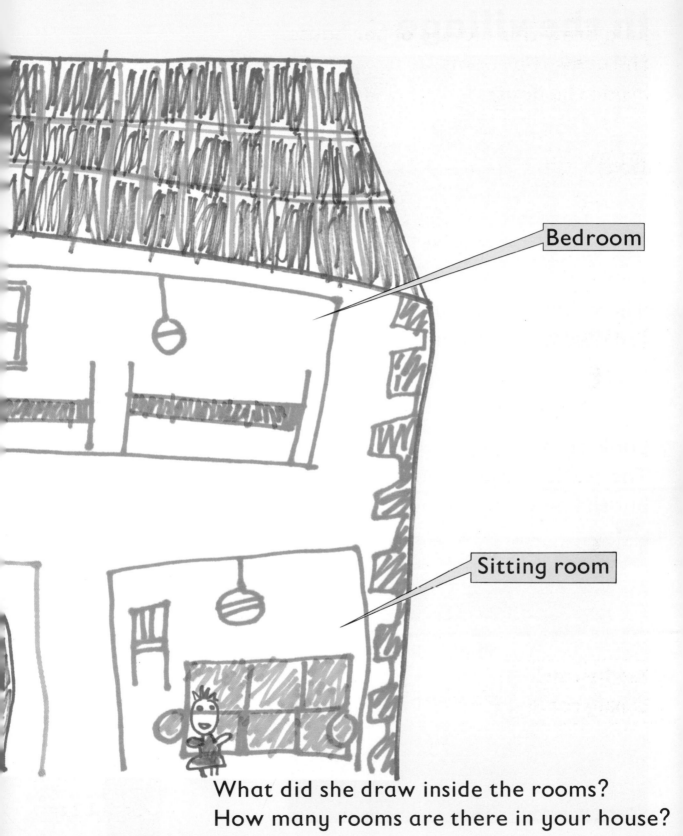

Bedroom

Sitting room

What did she draw inside the rooms?
How many rooms are there in your house?

In the village

The village where Julia goes to school
is called Castle Camps.

Look at the sign.
The castle has gone now
but the moat is still there.

There are no shops
in Julia's village.
Castle Camps
has two shops.
One shop is a
post office and
general store.

The other shop belongs
to the village butcher.
He sells meat.
What else does he sell?

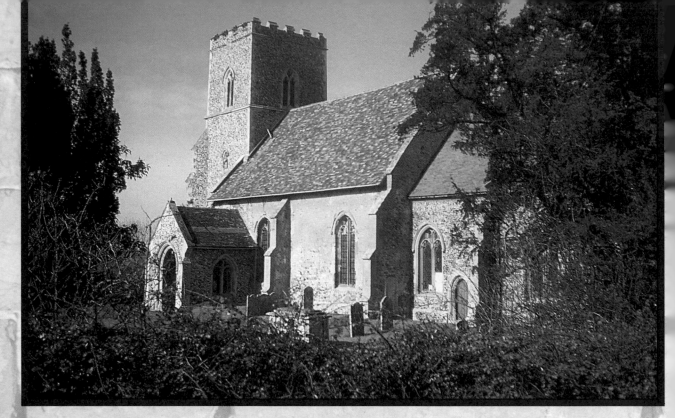

This is the old church in Castle Camps.
It is near the place where the castle used to stand.

Castle Camps also has a chapel.

There are some old houses
in Castle Camps.

They are in the middle
of the village.

On the edge of the village
there are newer houses.
Castle Camps is growing
all the time.

This is Castle Camps School.

Julia's class did a project on the village.
What can you see in the picture?

On the farm

There is a farm
near Julia's house.
It has a riding school.
Julia often comes here
for a riding lesson.

The ponies walk and trot
around this field. They
wear away the grass.

Julia often visits her friend Rebecca.
She lives on a farm too.
Rebecca has a donkey.

Julia and Rebecca like to run
in the fields.
The donkey follows them.

Cows also live on Rebecca's farm. They eat the grass in the fields. These cows give us milk. Butter, cheese and yoghurt are made from milk.

The cows are milked every day.

The milk goes to the dairy where it is put into bottles and crates. What happens next?

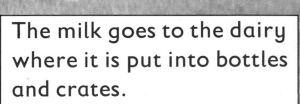

Wheat, barley and potatoes grow on the farm.
Wheat and barley are called grain crops.
When the grain is ripe it is a golden colour.

This machine is cutting the ripe wheat.
It is a combine harvester.

Wheat is made into bread.

This picture shows a crop of barley and a crop of potatoes growing in a field.

Potatoes grow on the roots of a plant.
They are called a root crop.
You can see the roots of a potato plant in this picture.
Can you think of other crops which grow on farms?
Would you like to visit a farm?

Index